MW00711703

SERMON OUTLINES
on

Selected Psalms

The Wood Sermon Outline Series

Sermon Outlines on Comfort and Assurance
Sermon Outlines on Coming to Christ
Sermon Outlines on the Easter Season
Sermon Outlines for Evangelistic Services
Sermon Outlines for Expository Preaching
Sermon Outlines for Funeral Services
Sermon Outlines on Gospel Passages
Sermon Outlines on Great Doctrinal Themes
Sermon Outlines on Men of the Bible
Sermon Outlines on the Names and Character of God
Sermon Outlines on the Old Testament
Sermon Outlines on Talks for Teens
Sermon Outlines on Practical Christian Living
Sermon Outlines on Prayer
Sermon Outlines on Proverbs
Sermon Outlines on Selected Psalms
Sermon Outlines on the Sermon on the Mount
Sermon Outlines for Special Days and Occasions, vol. 1
Sermon Outlines for Special Days and Occasions, vol. 2
Sermon Outlines on Spiritual Renewal
Sermon Outlines on Women of the Bible

SERMON OUTLINES

on

Selected Psalms

Charles R. Wood

kregel
PUBLICATIONS

Grand Rapids, MI 49501

Sermon Outlines on Selected Psalms

© 1986 by Charles R. Wood

Published by Kregel Publications, a division of Kregel, Inc.,
P.O. Box 2607, Grand Rapids, MI 49501. Kregel Publications
provides trusted, biblical publications for Christian growth and
service. Your comments and suggestions are valued.

For more information about Kregel Publications, visit our web
site at: www.kregel.com

Cover design: Frank Gutbrod

Library of Congress Cataloging-in-Publication
Sermon outlines on selected Psalms / by Charles R. Wood.
         p.   cm.
1. Bible. O.T. Psalms—Sermons—Outlines, syllabi, etc.
I. Title. II. Charles R. Wood.
BS1430.4W66   1985   85-23735
251'.02—dc20

ISBN 0-8254-4125-0

1 2 3 4 5 / 04 03 02 01 00

Printed in the United States of America

Contents

Introduction 7
What in the World? (Psalm 2) 9
He Giveth His Beloved Sleep (Psalm 3) 11
An Instructive Prayer (Psalm 5) 13
Because We Are Human (Psalm 6) 15
The Response of an Innocent Heart (Psalm 7) 17
What Is Man? (Psalm 8:4-6) 19
When the Lights Go Out (Psalm 10:1) 20
How God Sees Good Christianity (Psalm 15) 22
The Lord Hear Thee in the Day of Trouble (Psalm 20) 24
Where Did You Get What You Have? (Psalm 24:1, 2) 26
How To Overcome Insecurity (Psalm 26) 28
In the Time of Trouble (Psalm 27) 30
The Thankful Heart (Psalm 33) 32
A Psalm for Troubled Times (Psalm 33) 33
Turn Off That Alarm Clock (Psalm 46) 34
Who Is in Charge Here? (Psalm 50:15) 36
What Now? (Psalm 51:13) 37
Almighty God, C.P.A. (Psalms 56:8, 147:4) 39
Prayers God Does Not Answer (Psalm 66:18) 40
The Blessing of God (Psalm 67) 42
It Does Not Seem To Be Fair! (Psalm 73:1-17) 44
Skating on Thin Ice (Psalm 73:18-20) 45
The Aftermath of Doubt (Psalm 73:21-28) 46
The Joy of Serving Jesus (Psalm 100:2) 47
Thanksgiving (Psalm 103:1-5) 49
The Mercy of God (Psalm 103:8-18) 51
The Value of the Word (Psalm 119) 53
Cleansing a Young Man's Way (Psalm 119:9-11) 54
What To Do When You Are Lied About (Psalm 119:69) 56

The God Who Is There (Psalm 139:1-12).....................58
Comprehensive Knowledge (Psalm 139:1-6) 60
The Presence of God (Psalm 139:7-12).......................62
Thanks for the Memories (Psalm 145:7) 64

Introduction

The days of turbulence, sudden change and constant tension in which we live demand some clear voice which can give direction for living and also speak peace to the troubled soul seeking to survive. The Psalms provide just what is needed. Written by a number of different authors over a significant period of time, they speak to us today, as if they were written by modern men living in the present age.

Running the full gamut of human emotions from praise to despair, they show their authors for what they were — men of like passions such as we — and in the process explore the moods, fears, exultations, discouragements, triumphs, and tears of us all. How many times have we gone to the Psalms in time of distress, seeking solace, only to find the exact feelings we were experiencing revealed in the words of a Psalmist? How many times have we turned to them with hearts bursting with praise and adoration to God for some great goodness, only to find, again, that our very emotions are expressed for us in ways we could hardly duplicate?

Truly the Psalms are a book for today. Preaching from the Psalms will be of great benefit to any congregation, because they touch on the many realities of living and give expression to the unexpressed and inexpressible thoughts and emotions of God's people. Certainly the necessary study involved in taking the printed page of the Psalms and making the message live and burn in one's own heart will be well rewarded.

These messages are expository in nature, designed to open the Scriptures in such a way that their own message is plain and that they speak for themselves. Many of the Psalms are written so that they outline themselves. An attempt has been made to capture those outlines on paper and to develop them to the fullest extent possible in a brief compass.

The preacher who will take the time to study these outlines with his Bible open before him will find the time spent amply rewarded both in his own personal growth and in the benefit to those to whom he preaches. Many times a particular portion (or even one point) of an outline will suggest another message, and it is altogether possible that the outlines contained in this book could expand into two or three times as many messages. Thus a primary purpose of a book like this — to feed the mill of one's own thinking — would have been achieved.

As in all the books in this series, the sermons contained herein have been preached to the congregations of the local churches the compiler has been privileged to serve as pastor during the course of a ministry now spanning more than twenty five years. Thus they have been tried and proven effective. May the backing of prayer, the power of the Holy Spirit, the benefit of study and the fervor of a heart burning to communicate truth combine to make them useful in the ministry of countless others.

WHAT IN THE WORLD?

PSALM 2

INTRODUCTION:
Books go out of date quickly, but the Bible is unique in that it never goes out of date. It speaks to the very conditions that we see today. Four questions will show how this chapter applies to today.

I. **WHAT IS GOING ON IN THE WORLD? (1-3)**
   - A. General tumult (international, national, and personal)
   - B. Tumult is deliberate (2)
   - C. Tumult is purposive (An act of rebellion) (3)
   - D. Tumult is productive

II. **HOW DOES GOD VIEW ALL THIS? (4-6)**
   - A. He endures with derisive tolerance (there is something absurd in sin)
   - B. He interferes in their efforts
   - C. He stands upon absolute certainty—holy hill of Zion—supreme place in Jerusalem
   - D. He allows us a view of His operations

III. **HOW DOES CHRIST VIEW ALL THIS? (7-9)**
   (He is the one against whom all this is directed)
   - A. Sees Himself with the divine right of rule
   - B. Sees Himself as promised a dominion
   - C. Sees Himself as having the authority to act
   - D. Reiterates the claim of God to power

IV. **HOW SHOULD MAN REACT TO ALL THESE THINGS? (10-12)**
   - A. A call to wisdom
   - B. A call for surrender
   - C. A call for recognition

CONCLUSION:
We can have:
1. confident security: restful trust/trustful rest
2. amused detachment: do not take the world too seriously
3. hopeful expectation: anticipation of His reign
4. studied piety: someone so great has the right to rule
5. steady witness: ought to tell people what we know
6. thoughtful acceptance: complete surrender to His will

HE GIVETH HIS BELOVED SLEEP

PSALM 3

INTRODUCTION:

The Psalms were songs in their original form, sung to express some feeling or to tell about some event. This is a Psalm designed to tell about feelings in the face of an event.

I. **ITS CIRCUMSTANTIAL NECESSITY (1, 2)**
   A. Its historical setting: the rebellion of Absalom
   B. Its interesting details
      1. "How are they increased...." (2 Samuel 15:4, 5, 12)
      2. "Many there are that rise...." (2 Samuel 17:1, 24)
      3. "Many there be which say...." (2 Samuel 16:7, 8; 17:1-4)
   C. Its practical implications
      1. David faced a tremendous trial
      2. If ever a man had reason to be upset!

II. **ITS ENCOURAGING NATURE (3, 4)**
   A. Its changed viewpoint (3)
      1. Looking at the enemy (trouble); now at the Lord
      2. God became to him just what he needed: He also will for us
   B. Its specific provisions (3)
      1. Shield: provided needed protection
      2. Glory: the glory of the Lord made up for all loss
      3. Lifter up of my head: the one who takes away troubles
   C. Its experimental assurance: "I cried...He heard...." (4)

III. **ITS CONFIDENT RESULTS (5, 6)**
   A. Its internal calm (5)
      1. Peaceful sleep: out under the stars
      2. Safe awakening
      3. Reason: the Lord sustained me, kept me safe, and gave me sleep
   B. Its fear-defeating release (6)
      1. Note the expression of confidence
      2. Note the picturesque form

C. Its important implications
1. Deliverance had not yet come
2. Ultimately deliverance did come

IV. ITS ADEQUATE BASIS (7, 8)
A. Its accomplished aspects (7)
B. Its searching limitation (8)
1. "Salvation is of the Lord": it pertains to God alone to save
2. His *blessings* are for *His* people
C. Its suggested interrogation
1. Do you have this kind of confidence in the Lord?
2. Are you one of His people, so that you can know His blessings?

CONCLUSION:
We all face trials. We all need David's confidence in Divine protection in the midst of them. He looked to God; He knew what God had promised; and He drew on the promises of God. You have to be a child of God before these things go into action for you.

AN INSTRUCTIVE PRAYER

PSALM 5

INTRODUCTION:
We do not know the situation of this Psalm, but it was a time of deep trouble. It was similar to what Christianity in general and many individual Christians face today.

I. **ITS STATED DETERMINATION (1-3)**
    A. "Unto thee will I pray" (2b)
    B. Request for audience (1, 2a)
    C. The indicated time (3)

II. **ITS ASSURED CONFIDENCE (4-6)**
    A. Known factors in God's character (three pairs)
        1. No pleasure at all in wickedness (4a)
            Hates (with a righteous hatred) all workers of evil (5b)
        2. No evil shall be thy guest (4b)
            Thou shalt destroy them that speak lies (6a)
        3. The foolish shall not stand in thy sight (5a)
            The Lord will abhor the bloody and deceitful (6b)
    B. The conviction of the correctness of own cause
    C. The explicit warning to the unconverted

III. **ITS CONTRASTING INTENTION (7)**
    A. David's intention: "But as for me...."
    B. The contrast shown

IV. **ITS SPECIFIC REQUESTS (8-12)**
    A. For himself (8, 9)
        1. His desire (8)
        2. His reasons (9)
    B. For his enemies (10)
        1. His desire (10a)
        2. His reasons (10b)
    C. For all the other people of God (11, 12)
        1. His desire: "rejoice", "shout for joy", "be joyful in God"

2. His reasons: "thou defendest them", "thou dost bless the righteous", "thou dost protect the righteous"
3. The condition: "put their trust in Thee", "them also that love thy name", "the righteous"

CONCLUSION:

Here is a most instructive prayer. Oh, that it might make some wise unto salvation and encourage others to trust in the Lord.

BECAUSE WE ARE HUMAN

PSALM 6

INTRODUCTION:
There is a saying, "He is only human." It is a profound truth, and God knows it well (Ps. 103:14). The Bible clearly takes it into account and speaks of it! This Psalm tells us about ourselves and our reactions.

I. **A COMMON EMOTION (1)**
   A. The problem of guilt
   B. How to handle the emotion
      1. Expect some chastisement
      2. Recognize that not all problems are punishment
      3. Check to see what God is doing

II. **A CORRELATION EFFECT (2b, 3)**
   A. All of life affected
      1. The physical and the emotional both involved: "bones", "soul", "vexed"
      2. Psychological upset becomes so great it affects the physical
   B. This is significant for the Christian
      1. Ordering our lives by the Bible might change our physical situation because of changed emotions
      2. Biblical living is designed to make life worth living

III. **A CLEAR-CUT EXAMPLE (4-7)**
   A. Depression and worry affect the Psalmist
      1. Make him feel forsaken of God (4)
      2. Make him fear death (5)
      3. Make him continually grieve (6)
      4. Make him react physically (7)
   B. This is significant for the Christian
      1. Depression knocks life off center
      2. Depression closes the door to God's blessings
      3. The Christian need not yield to depressive tendencies

15

IV. A CHALLENGING ENCOURAGEMENT (2a, 4, 8-10)
   A. Take problems to the Lord
   B. How to find help from God
      1. Recognize our weakness (2a)
      2. Realize His mercy (4)
      3. Request His help
   C. How God helps us (8-10)
      1. He changes our viewpoint
      2. He gives us assurance
      3. He strengthens us to endure trials
      4. He delivers us out of troubles

CONCLUSION:
   We are human; therefore, we have troubles. We must handle them and not turn to the wrong place for help. So much is a matter of proper relationship to the Lord, which determines what you do to troubles and what troubles do to you!

THE RESPONSE OF
AN INNOCENT HEART

PSALM 7

INTRODUCTION:
It is difficult to be accused when innocent. It is even more difficult to be persecuted when righteous or doing righteously. David's situation and reaction on this score are interesting.

I.   **HIS PRAYER (1, 2)**
   A. Statement of trust
   B. Request for help (desire for deliverance)
   C. Basic attitude involved in verse 10

II.   **THE BASIS OF HIS PRAYER: AN INNOCENT HEART (3-5)**
   A. Specific examinations
       1. "If I have done this" (what he was accused of doing)
       2. "If there is any blood on my hands"
       3. "If I have rewarded evil to one at peace with me"
       4. "If I have even done in my enemy"
   B. Willingness for penalty: let his worst desires come true

III.   **THE CONTENTS OF HIS PRAYER (6, 7)**
   A. Get angry, Lord
   B. Lift Thyself up in judgment
   C. Rise up on Thy throne

IV.   **THE CONFIDENCE OF HIS PRAYER (8-13)**
   A. The Lord shall judge the peoples (8)
   B. The righteous judge trieth the minds and hearts (9)
   C. God judges the righteous, but He is angry with the wicked (11)
   D. God will only put up with so much wickedness (12, 13)

V.   **THE CAUSE OF HIS PRAYER (14, 15)**
   A. His enemy is ripely full of iniquity

B. He has conceived mischief, germinated and given birth to dishonesty
C. He has prepared a trap for me

VI. THE ASSURANCE OF THE PRAYER
A. God is a defense and a good one—He saveth the upright in heart (10)
B. God allows my enemies to fall into their own traps (15)
C. The righteousness of God gives me great confidence in Him (17)

CONCLUSION:

There are so many lessons here. In time of attack, David turns to God! It takes a very right heart to say what verses 3-5 express!

WHAT IS MAN?

PSALM 8:4-6

INTRODUCTION:
There are certain questions that have been asked for generations that seem to defy any solid answer, but the Bible provides the answers. In Psalm 8 it asks: "What is man?" and then goes on to provide the answers.

I.   **MAN IS THE APEX OF GOD'S CREATION**
     ("Thou has made him....,visa")
     A. He bears God's image and likeness (4b)
     B. He is made just a little lower than the angels (5a)
     C. He is crowned, by God, with glory and honor (6-8)

II. **THE CAUSE OF GOD'S HEARTBREAK**
     A. Man marred the likeness of God
        1. Unholy instead of holy
        2. Unrighteous rather than righteous
        3. Untrue instead of true
        4. Unfaithful instead of faithful
        5. Rebellious instead of obedient
     B. Man became self exalting
        1. Was designed to give praise to God
        2. Promotes himself at every opportunity
     C. Man distorted the dominion God gave him
        1. Misread it to indicate that he could waste the earth rather than just dominate it
        2. Everything he has touched shows the impress of his hand in some negative way

III. **THE OBJECT OF GOD'S AFFECTION**
     A. God has him in mind
     B. God has chosen to visit him
     C. God has made provision for his needs

CONCLUSION:
What is man? A self created mess! A mess that has broken God's heart! A mess for which God has made provision! Have you found that provision?

WHEN THE LIGHTS GO OUT

PSALM 10:1

INTRODUCTION:
All is going well; then suddenly problems begin to develop. They grow larger and steadily more involved. At length they grow so large that they blot out the sun, and life becomes hopelessly gray and foreboding. The LIGHTS HAVE GONE OUT. When they do, there are some things to remember:

I.   **THIS IS A COMMON EXPERIENCE**
    A. Psalmist experienced an upset
        1. Felt that something had happened to his relationship with God
        2. Fairly common experience for David (Ps. 13:1; 22:1, 11, 19; 35:22, 23; 38:21, 22; 55:1; 71:12)
    B. We share the same experiences
        1. Everything is just too much
        2. Spiritual manifestations of being forsaken of God most common

II. **THIS CAUSES US TO LOSE PERSPECTIVE**
    A. Illustrated by Elijah's experience (1 Kings 19:1-4)
        1. Elijah has known triumph
        2. He was likely drained emotionally and physically
        3. He lost his perspective
    B. Application
        1. There are various causes for the lights going out
        2. This has its effects upon us in many ways

III. **THIS IS A PROBLEM IN APPEARANCE ONLY**
    A. Illustrated (2 Kings 6:13-17)
        1. The city surrounded by a great company
        2. Young man was afraid, but Elisha showed him something
    B. Applied
        1. We tend to focus on trouble
        2. We need to remember the promise of God "Lo, I am with you ALWAYS"

IV. **THIS IS OFTEN FOLLOWED BY A REVELATION OF HIS PERSON**
   A. Illustrated (Luke 24:13-31)
      1. Time of darkest night for disciples
      2. Both their Messiah and their hopes were dead
      3. He reveals Himself to them in their misery
   B. Applied
      1. God has promised to deliver us — when things get bleakest, the break must come
      2. We should thus be encouraged in trials

V. **THIS REMINDS US OF WHAT CHRIST SUFFERED**
   A. Illustrated (Mark 15:33-35)
      1. He knew separation
      2. He suffered infinitely under it, and cried out in the midst of it
   B. Applied
      1. We can be sure He knows what our trial is like
      2. We can sense something of His agony

CONCLUSION:

When the lights go out, remember: it is a common experience. It causes us to lose perspective. It is only a problem in appearance. It is usually followed by a great revelation. It reminds us of what He suffered.

HOW GOD SEES GOOD CHRISTIANITY

PSALM 15

INTRODUCTION:
Almost everyone wants to be a good Christian. The way to do so is a matter of controversy. Here is helpful information.

I.   **HOW WE JUDGE A GOOD CHRISTIAN**
    A. Criteria: Spiritual, sincere, godly, sweet, interested, kind, etc.
    B. Note subjective tendency in so much

II.   **HOW GOD SEES A GOOD CHRISTIAN**
    A. The question: "Lord, who gets close to You?" (1)
    B. The answer (2-5a)
       1. A very specific list
       2. Stress on character
    C. The summation (5)
       1. The man like this has it
       2. This man shall stand firm

III. **THE SPECIFICS FOR WHICH GOD LOOKS**
    A. "He that walketh uprightly": walk refers to all of life
    B. "He that worketh righteousness": actions in accord with profession
    C. "He that speakest the truth in his heart": truth in the heart will show by truth on the lips
    D. "He that backbiteth not with his tongue": to speak behind one's back
    E. "He that doeth not evil to his neighbor"
    F. "He that taketh not up a reproach against his neighbor": does not take up on what he has heard
    G. "In whose eyes a vile person is condemned"
    H. "He honoreth them that fear the Lord": "in honor preferring one another"
    I.   "He sweareth to his own hurt and changeth not" basic reference to keeping His word
    J. "He putteth not out his money to usury": excessive interest rates to make money at expense of others

K. "Nor taketh reward against the innocent": will have no part in that which takes from the innocent

IV.   THE BLESSING GOD GIVES (5b)
"He that doeth these things shall never be moved": stability (sin causes instability)

CONCLUSION:
Would God call you a good Christian?

THE LORD HEAR THEE IN THE DAY OF TROUBLE

PSALM 20

INTRODUCTION:
(Use responsive reading of the Psalm as it may have been done in the Tabernacle in the days of David. People read first five verses. Pastor reads verses 6-8. Unison on verse 9.)

I. **THE BACKGROUND OF THE PSALM**
    A. Psalm written to be used before a battle
    B. Probably done in responsive reading style and gave all the people an opportunity to participate in preparations for war
    C. Probably accompanied a special offering of sacrifice in request of God's favor

II. **THE CONTENT OF THE PSALM**
    A. General
       1. In the form of a prayer
       2. Makes great case out of the "name of God" concept (cf. vv. 2, 5, 7)
    B. Specific
       1. Calls upon the "God of Jacob" because Jacob was in and out of so much trouble that those thinking of him would think in terms of deliverance from trouble (1)
       2. The Psalmist asks for help from the place of God's visible presence and gets help out of heaven itself (2, 6)
       3. "Grant thee the wishes of thine heart and make all your plans to succeed" (4)
       4. "Salvation" here is not the usual spiritual sense but rather that of deliverance (5)
       5. The Lord saves the one chosen of Him: the Lord takes care of His own (6)
       6. Some trust in physical might, but we will continue to place our confidence in the Lord God (7)
       7. "Lord, save the King"—a special prayer for the leader in the time of battle (9)

III. THE APPLICATIONS OF THE PASSAGE
    A. In case of trouble, Pray
    B. In the face of trouble, perform regular spiritual obligations
    C. In the face of trouble, trust the Lord
    D. If there are victories won by God's people in trouble, God will win them

CONCLUSION:
God has made provision for His people. Trust Him in time of trial. The God of Jacob will deliver.

WHERE DID YOU GET WHAT YOU HAVE?

PSALM 24:1, 2

INTRODUCTION
We do not do well in recognizing cause/effect relationships. We are especially poor at recognizing where we got what we have.

I. **EXPRESSION**
    A. Everything in world belongs to God (Ps. 50:10-12; 104:24)
    B. God has the absolute right of control over all things
    C. God allows man a measure of freedom
    D. Man can stand and grapple with God over that beautiful thing called God's plan for life

II. **EXAMPLES**
    (Many Bible characters wrestled with God and paid dearly)
    A. Adam
    B. Abraham
    C. Isaac
    D. Jacob
    E. Moses
    F. Saul
    G. David
    H. Jonah
    I. Demas

III. **EXPLANATIONS**
    A. Problem
       1. God has a will and a right to have it
       2. His will is best for us
       3. We stubbornly fight it
    B. Symptoms
       1. Sporadic and irregular church attendance
       2. Inconsistent and undependable service
       3. Occasional and casual devotion
       4. Indifferent and half-hearted participation

CONCLUSION:

God made us and gave us all we have. God has a plan for us, and behind most of our rebellion, disobedience and failure lies lack of surrender to His will and His plan.

HOW TO OVERCOME INSECURITY

PSALM 26

INTRODUCTION:
Insecurity tends to move in one of two directions. It either makes a person inept and spineless or makes him compensate by becoming vocal and over-bearing. Psalm 26 was written to counter false accusations, but it is an interesting study in a man's security.

I. **STATEMENTS OF SECURITY**
   A. Listed
      1. I lead a blameless life (1, 11)
      2. I have not wavered (1)
      3. My feet are on level ground (12)
   B. Sounds like compensation: a weak, insecure man trying to sound strong by being brash

II. **SUPERLATIVES OF SECURITY**
   A. It is not brash — proved by what else he says
   B. Invites God to examine him (1, 2)
   C. Invites God to explore his claims. Instead of a brash, weak man, we have a genuinely secure man

III. **SUBSTANCE OF SECURITY**
   A. He trusted in the Lord: "I have trusted also in the Lord" (1)
   B. He knew something about the Lord in whom he trusted: "Thy loving kindness is before mine eyes" (3)
   C. He was living obediently: "I have walked in thy truth" (3)
   D. He was blessing the Lord: "In the congregations will I bless the Lord" (12)

IV. **SPECIFICS OF SECURITY**
   A. Separation from evil (4, 5)
   B. Dealing with sin (6)
   C. Proper spiritual activity (7, 8)

V. SUPPLICATION OF SECURITY (9, 10)
   A. Redeem me: buy me back from sin's hold (11)
   B. Be merciful to me (11)
   C. Keep me from wrong people (9, 10)

CONCLUSION:

David was, at least at this place, genuinely secure. How did he get that way? God was his confidence! He learned who God was and what He could do and lived biblically. There is no magic cure for insecurity; security comes as we do things God's way.

IN THE TIME OF TROUBLE

PSALM 27

INTRODUCTION:
The ups and downs in problems are not unique to us. David knew the same thing. David's temporary instability did not prevent him from receiving God's help (God understands, Ps. 103:14). The only thing that will finally see us through our troubles is confidence in God's ability to see us through.

I. **THE EXPRESSION OF PRAISE (1-3)**
    A. God's person (1)
        1. He is three things to me
            a. Light: the one that illumines my darkness
            b. Salvation: from sin and trouble
            c. Strength (or defense): someone to hide behind
        2. Which means two things to me (Rom. 8:31)
            a. I need not fear: the specific and known
            b. I need not dread: the vague and the unknown
    B. God's protection (2)
    C. God's provision (3)

II. **EVALUATION OF PROBLEMS (4-12)**
    A. Purpose: Statement of His own personal desires (4-6)
        1. Desire (4)
        2. Design: the reasons He desires to be in the house of the Lord (5)
        3. Declaration (6)
    B. Petition: then He turns to prayer (7-12)
        1. Request (7, 8)
        2. Reassurance: He deeply senses His need of some word of reassurance (9)
        3. Reaffirmation: Closes His prayer by reaffirming his confidence in God (10)

III. **EXHORTATION TO PATIENCE (13, 14)**
    A. Assurance (13)
        1. Something has kept him from despair
        2. That something is the conviction that he is going to come out right

B. Exhortations (14)
    1. Be strong and let your heart take courage
    2. Wait on the Lord
       a. Wait at His door with prayer
       b. Wait at His feet with humility
       c. Wait at His table with service
       d. Wait at His window with expectancy

CONCLUSION:

Look to the Lord in the time of trouble. Follow the "waiting" procedure.

THE THANKFUL HEART

PSALM 33

INTRODUCTION:
Thanksgiving is such a familiar theme that it turns trite. A new look at the word may help us see it afresh.

I.   **AN EXHORTATION TO PRAISE (1-3)**
     A. Praise is fit: befitting or comely
     B. Praise may involve instruments
     C. Praise should involve a new song

II.   **SOME REASONS FOR PRAISE (4-19)**
     A. God's general character (4, 5)
     B. God's wisdom and power shown in creation (6-9)
     C. God's truly stable purposes (10, 11)
     D. God's blessings on those who acknowledge Him as God (12-19)

III.   **AN INTENTION TO PRAISE (20-22)**
     A. "We will wait on the Lord": depending or looking for intervention (20)
     B. "Our hearts shall rejoice in Him": our trust in Him is an occasion of joy (21)
     C. "Let Thy mercy be upon us as we trust in Thee": mercy is conditioned by our hope in Him (22)

CONCLUSION:
There is so much for which to praise God that thanksgiving should never become trite. Are you praising?

A PSALM FOR TROUBLED TIMES

PSALM 33

INTRODUCTION:

We face many problems in the troubled times in which we live. In all of them, however, it is possible to maintain our spiritual equilibrium and to be rejoicing, triumphant Christians.

I.   **THE CHALLENGE (1-3)**
    A. Contained in three words: rejoice, praise, sing
    B. The object of them all is the Lord
    C. We are even given specific directions
        1. Praise is a fitting garment for the upright
        2. Our praise should be a growing thing ("new")

II. **THE CAUSE (4-19)**
    A. The communication of the Lord: His Word (4a)
    B. The conduct of God (4b)
    C. The character of the Lord (5a)
    D. The compassion of the Lord (5b)
    E. The creation of the Lord (6-9)
    F. The counsel of the Lord (10, 11)
    G. The care of the Lord (12-19)

III. **THE COMMITMENT (20-22)**
    A. We must wait for the Lord
    B. We must see Him as our provision
    C. Trusting in Him will bring sure rejoicing

CONCLUSION:

Look at what our Lord is and does! Rejoice, praise, sing, TRUST! If His mercy is according to our hope, we had better get our heads up and take fast hold of hope!

TURN OFF THAT ALARM CLOCK!

PSALM 46

INTRODUCTION:

We live in an "alarm" society. Everyone seems to be clamoring, and everything clanging. Many of us face personal problems of various types that ring like gigantic "alarm clocks". It seems as if this is a time when the devil is working overtime to disturb God's people and cause us to fear. God's Word in Psalm 46 says, "turn off that alarm clock".

I. **THE STRUCTURE OF THE PSALM**
    A. It is a hymn with three clearly marked stanzas: 1-3; 4-7; 8-11
    B. It was written to be sung as part of the temple worship

II. **THE SETTING OF THE PSALM**
    A. Probably describes a situation in 2 Kings 18 & 19
    B. The writer reviews and applies what had happened and what had been learned

III. **THE STATEMENT OF THE PSALM (1-3)**
    A. The reality
       1. God is our refuge: the place to go for protection
       2. God is our strength
       3. God is our help: the One Who comes to our aid and assistance
    B. The result
       1. We will not fear (statement of the will)
       2. Even though terrible things happen in nature
       3. We will not fear no matter how bad things get

IV. **THE SUPPORT OF THE PSALM (4-7)**
    A. Protection (4)
    B. Presence: here is why there is peace (5)
    C. Power (6)
    D. Promise (7)

V. THE SIGNIFICANCE OF THE PSALM (8-11)

A. Invitation: come, behold, review what God has done ("desolations"- over-throws of men and nations) (8)

B. Identifications (9)
1. He maketh wars to cease
2. Breaketh bow/cutteth spear: makes them useless
3. Burneth war chariots

C. Implication (10, 11)
1. Be still, calm, restful, trustful: "let your hand sink down"
2. And know that I am God — see the evidence in what has already been said and done to believe that I am God
3. I will be exalted — rest assured. I will show myself strong in be half of My people

CONCLUSION:

Let the worst come to the worst. A child of God need never give way to mistrust. Since God is faithful, there can be no danger to His cause or people.

WHO IS IN CHARGE HERE?

PSALM 50:15

INTRODUCTION:
Some people go through troubles very well. One such was Andrew Murray, the "South African prayer warrior." This is his secret of success.

I. **MY POSITION**
   A. He brought me here
   B. It is by His will that I am in this place
   C. In this I can rest

II. **GOD'S PROVISION**
   A. He will keep me here in His love
   B. He will give me grace in this trial to behave as His child
   C. I can also be sure I will not be called upon to handle more than I am capable of handling

III. **GOD'S PURPOSES**
   A. He will make the trial a blessing
   B. This blessing will be shown in two specific ways
      1. By teaching me the lessons He intends me to learn
      2. By working in me the grace which He means to bestow

IV. **MY PROMOTION**
   A. He will bring me out again
   B. He knows the details

V. **MY PROPOSITION**
   A. I am here
      1. By God's appointment
      2. In His keeping
      3. Under His training
      4. For His time
   B. I will use this time wisely

CONCLUSION:
What a wonderful assurance in every time of trial and hardship. How it ought to change our lives!

WHAT NOW?

PSALM 51:13

INTRODUCTION:
The real test of a church is what it does on a week to week basis when the pressure is off and the special emphasis is over. Interesting little verse in Psalm 51 has a long story behind it. Look at the story and at the verse and then see how it applies.

I.   **A SAD STORY**
A. Read 2 Samuel 11
    1. Note David's sin
    2. Note that David set himself to cover the whole matter
B. Psalm 32:3, 4 describes what went on in David's mind and heart during the time of unrepentance
C. Read 2 Samuel 12:1-15a
    1. Notice God's exposure of the sin
    2. Notice David's repentant state
D. Psalm 51 describes what happened after David was willing to face and deal with his sin

II. **A STRONG STATEMENT**
A. Explained
    1. David has been out of fellowship with the Lord
    2. He has been through a period of revival
    3. Now he says: I am ready to see people get right with God, now that I am right with Him
B. Expressed
    1. When we are really right with God, souls will be saved as a result
    2. When souls are not being saved, it is a sign that there is something wrong

III. **A SCRIPTURAL SUPPORT**
A. Acts 1:8 speaks of witnessing and winning the lost as being absolutely natural for the Christian
B. Proverbs 24:11, 12
    1. Failure to warn others is inexcusable
    2. Failure to warn others has sure retribution

C. Ezekiel 3:17-21
   1. If we know the danger—and we do—and fail to warn, the blood of those thus lost will be required at our hands
   2. The response of people is not our obligation; warning them is
D. Acts 20:25-27
   Paul says that he is clear of the blood of all men as he faithfully warned of everything he knew

CONCLUSION:
If you are not doing what you can to warn others, there is something wrong spiritually. If you are not warning, you are in jeopardy.

ALMIGHTY GOD, C.P.A.

PSALMS 56:8; 147:4

INTRODUCTION:
God is interested in numbers; in fact, He is the ultimate accountant.

I. **THERE ARE THINGS WHICH GOD KEEPS COUNT OF**
   A. The number of His people (Book of Numbers)
   B. The people who are added to that total (Book of Acts)
   C. The labor invested in seeking to bring people to God
   D. Any labor of love and work of faith (Hebrews 6:10)

II. **THERE ARE THINGS WHICH GOD KEEPS NO COUNT OF (OR STRIKES FROM THE RECORD)**
   A. Sins which have been forgiven (Ps. 103:13)
   B. Failures in our lives (Ps. 103:14)
   C. The number of times we have tried before
   D. The terrible things we have done in our lives before turning to Him (Isa. 44:22)

CONCLUSION:
In the areas of your frustration, He remembers. In the areas of your failures, He forgets. Turn it over to Him.

PRAYERS GOD DOES NOT ANSWER

PSALM 66:18

INTRODUCTION:
God always hears prayer, but there are some prayers that He does not heed; therefore, they will not be answered. He is not obligated to answer these.

I. **THE ALREADY ANSWERED PRAYER**
    A. Prayers for things He has already answered in His Word
    B. Do not fail to pray: just pray for the right things

II. **THE HYPOCRITICAL PRAYER**
    A. When our lips speak other than what our heart means or wants
    B. Very common: thoughtless praying
    C. Our prayers must express what is really in our hearts in order to be heard by God

III. **THE UNBELIEVING PRAYER**
    A. From James 1:5-7
    B. From Mark 11:23, 24
    C. Two questions surface here:
        1. Did you really believe God could do it?
        2. Did you really expect God to do it?

IV. **THE RESENTFUL PRAYER**
    A. From Mark 11:23-25
        1. We may not expect God to give us what we will not give to another
        2. Bitterness, resentment, etc., form a serious and major barrier
    B. Biblical procedure outlines
        1. We are to forgive in our hearts at once (the example of Christ)
        2. We are to pursue any biblical procedure required (e.g., Matt. 15)

3. We are only to grant forgiveness on the basis of a repentant request (Luke 17:3)

CONCLUSION:

Before you decide the Lord has abandoned you, take time to review these things. Prayer is a great resource, but it is not the magic wand a lot of people want to make it.

THE BLESSING OF GOD

PSALM 67

INTRODUCTION:
A theme constantly repeated among us (we say, "God bless you", "God is so good," etc.). This little Psalm can teach us many things we do not know concerning the blessing of God.

I. **ITS PROCLAMATION**
    A. The mercy of God—all blessings begin with mercy—makes them meaningful (1)
    B. The prosperity of God (1, 6a)
        1. Word "bless" in verse 1
        2. All material blessings come from His hand: every good thing we have
    C. The presence of God (1)
        1. We have the presence of God in ultimate form in the incarnation
        2. We have His presence continually throughout life

II. **ITS PERSONALIZATION (6b)**
    A. A personal possession
        1. He possesses us: we belong to Him
        2. We possess Him: He belongs to us
    B. A personal relationship
        1. More than just the factual aspect of possession
        2. This enters into the realm of daily life
    C. Personal provision
        1. Whatever He sends me has a "customized" tag on it
        2. He is aware of my specific needs, wants, etc.

III. **ITS PURPOSE**
    A. Praise (3-5)
        1. We are to praise Him by what we say
        2. We are to praise Him by what we think
        3. We are to praise Him by how we live
    B. Proclamation (2, 7)

CONCLUSION:

How has God blessed you? How are you praising Him? How are you fulfilling the purposes of His blessing? The more blessings you have, the more obligation you are under to fulfill His purposes (talents, abilities, skills, money, personality, etc.)

IT DOES NOT SEEM TO BE FAIR!

PSALM 73:1-17

INTRODUCTION:

The good sometimes suffer privation. The wicked often totally escape retribution. This faces us with a problem concerning the goodness of God and the accuracy of God's Word. Asaph, who wrote Psalm 73, was also faced with this question and found a solution to it.

I. ASAPH'S CONVICTION REGARDING GOD (1)
A. God is good to Israel
B. This goodness to Israel is conditioned by a "clean heart"

II. THE WAY ASAPH ARRIVED AT HIS CONVICTION (2-17)
A. He did not always feel this way (2)
B. Observations had caused this trouble (3-9)
C. Asaph had weighed these things (10-16)
   1. This causes the righteous to wonder, and they end up questioning God (11)
   2. Then it causes the righteous to despair
   3. The whole thing became most painful (16)
D. Asaph found a solution to them (17)
   1. Finally turned to the Lord
   2. Found a satisfactory answer: they have not reached their end yet, but they will!

III. THE LESSONS WE NEED TO LEARN FROM THIS
A. When we are upset over the prosperity of the wicked, we are forgetting some things
B. When we are faced with great dilemmas and trials, we need to turn to the Lord instead of away from Him
C. Let us remember that the answers are with God and turn to Him to find them!

CONCLUSION:

This would be an ultimately unfair world were this world the end of all things. The answer lies in the coming judgment.

SKATING ON THIN ICE

PSALM 73:18-20

INTRODUCTION:
The evil man appears to prosper and that is most discouraging. The evil man, however, is skating on thin ice.

I.   THE IDENTIFICATION OF THE WICKED
   A. Broader than those who do flagrant wrong
   B. God has established a standard of judgment (John 3:36)

II.   THE ACTUAL STATE OF THE WICKED (18-20)
   A. They are set in slippery places (18a)
   B. They are viewed as already cast into destruction (20b)
   C. They are brought into desolation in a moment (19a)
   D. They are consumed with terrors (19b)
   E. They are as dreamers who must awaken to reality (20)

III.   THE HOPE OF THE WICKED
   A. God does not desire the destruction of the wicked
   B. The escape is provided

CONCLUSION:
The wicked man slides on thin ice. He needs the solidarity of salvation in Christ.

THE AFTERMATH OF DOUBT

PSALM 73:21-28

INTRODUCTION:
The Psalmist has been through a period of great doubt about the operation of God. Out of his doubt has come conviction:

I. **THE FOLLY OF PREVIOUS FEELINGS (21, 22)**
   A. The feelings described (21)
   B. The feelings analyzed (22)

II. **THE CERTAINTY OF GOD'S CONSTANCY (23, 24)**
   A. It has been great in the past (23)
   B. I am confident it will continue to be great (24)

III. **A SENSE OF SATISFACTION WITH GOD (25, 26)**
   A. God alone *can* satisfy (25)
      1. None in heaven but Him who can
      2. There is none on earth beside Him
      3. He is all that anyone needs
   B. God alone *will* satisfy
      1. Looks to a time when strength might fail
      2. Is assured of reaction then

IV. **CONVICTION THAT GOD HAS THE FINAL ANSWERS (27, 28)**
   A. All inequities of life will be righted (27)
   B. We must stay close to the Lord
   C. We must simply trust God

CONCLUSION:
Asaph climbed the mountain in the dark—now that the top is reached, he is resolved not to do it that way again.

THE JOY OF SERVING JESUS

PSALM 100:2

INTRODUCTION:
We sing, "There is joy in serving Jesus." We are commanded
to serve Him with gladness. Often we do not find much joy in
service. How can we serve the Lord with gladness?

I. **BE SURE IT IS THE LORD WE ARE SERVING**
    A. Wrong objects: Pastor, church, people, job
    B. Wrong motives: Self satisfaction, praise, recognition,
       fulfillment

II. **SPEND TIME WITH THE LORD BEFORE
    WORKING FOR THE LORD**
    A. Needs: direction, assurance, strength
    B. Means: Word of God, prayer, devotions

III. **DETERMINE WHAT IT IS THAT YOU ARE TO DO**
    A. Divided minds hamper joy
    B. Be sure you are doing what God wants you to do

IV. **GIVE WHAT YOU ARE DOING EVERYTHING
    YOU HAVE TO OFFER**
    A. Throw yourself into the task. The more you hold back,
       the less you enjoy
    B. If it is worth doing at all, it is worth doing well

V. **COMMIT YOURSELF TO SEE IT THROUGH**
    A. Do not quit and do not give up in weakness what you
       have taken on in strength
    B. Do not lay down something until God has given you
       something to take its place

VI. **CONCENTRATE ON THE TASK, NOT ON THE
    RESULTS**
    A. God measures success by faithfulness and effort
    B. Learn to find joy in the task in doing it and in
       knowing it is properly done.

VII. ADJUST YOUR FOCUS
   A. Seek to count the blessings
   B. Seek to increase your effectiveness
   C. Seek to minister to people
   D. Always look on the bright side

CONCLUSION:
There is joy in serving Jesus. These are the steps to take to insure it. Do you need to get back to the joy?

THANKSGIVING

PSALM 103:1-5

INTRODUCTION:
We complain, criticize and fuss when we ought to be expressing praise. It is unfortunate that we only concentrate on thanksgiving at one season of the year. We have enough to praise Him all year long.

I. **THE CALL TO PRAISE**
    A. "Bless the Lord" (1a) — praise the Lord
    B. "Oh my soul, and all that is within me" (1b) — from the innermost part of my being
    C. "Bless His holy name" (2a) — His character and all that He truly is
    D. "And forget not all His benefits" (2b) — all His dealings

II. **THE CONSIDERATIONS TO PRAISE**
    There are six reasons to praise Him here
    A, "Who forgiveth all thine iniquities" (3a)
    B. "Who healeth all thy diseases" (3b) — all but the last one
    C. "Who redeemeth thy life from destruction" (4a)
    D. "Who crowneth thee with lovingkindness and tender mercies" (4b)
    E. "Who satisfieth thy mouth with good things" (5a)
    F. "Thy youth is renewed like the eagle's" (5b)

III. **THE CHALLENGE TO PRAISE**
    A. We dare not forget to praise the Lord
    B. We must continually praise
    C. "What shall I render unto the Lord for all His benefits to me?" (Ps. 116:12)

CONCLUSION:
God has forgiven us, overpowered our enemies, turned our lives around, honored us, supplied all our needs and more, renovated us continually.

What will we do to show our gratitude?

THE MERCY OF GOD

PSALM 103:8-18

INTRODUCTION:
Have you ever done anything for which you really felt you deserved punishment, and it did not come? Then you know about God's mercy. There is much more than this to the mercy of God.

I. **THE DEFINITION OF MERCY**
   A. Has basic idea of pity (v. 13)
   B. God's attitude toward us in our misery
   C. The actions which spring from God's attitude toward us (v. 10)

II. **THE DEMAND FOR MERCY**
   A. Our miserable condition
   B. Our misery stems from our sinful humanity (14-16)
   C. Our misery shows itself in various ways
      1. The lack of truthfulness: politics, philosophy, religion
      2. The lack of faithfulness: friends, associates, etc.
      3. The lack of justice: unrighted wrongs, prosperity of wicked

III. **THE DEMONSTRATION OF MERCY**
   A. God meets us in the place and point of our need
   B. God shows His mercy in specific ways
   C. God's actions and attitudes toward us are for our ultimate good

IV. **THE DANGER OF MERCY**
   A. Longsuffering is basic part of mercy (v. 8)
   B. Longsuffering has its limits (v. 9)
      1. Disobedient Christian: God's mercy keeps things from happening which could
      2. Unsaved sinner: there is a line which can be crossed

V. THE DESIGN OF MERCY
   A. To bring us into conformity with Him
   B. To bring us out of our misery

CONCLUSION:
It is because of mercy we are not consumed. Are you pushing His mercy? It has limits. What makes it frightening is that we do not know where the limits are.

THE VALUE OF THE WORD

PSALM 119

INTRODUCTION:
The Bible's worth is declared by most all. It has always had enormous value to God's people, and this psalm shows the reason why.

I. **IT HAS CLEANSING POWER**
   A. Power to keep from defilement (1-3)
   B. Power to render clean (9-11)

II. **IT IS A STOREHOUSE OF GOOD THINGS**
   A. Its content is good
      1. It contains wondrous things (18)
      2. Its truths are delights and counselors (24)
      3. Its teaching lets us see fantastic things (18)
   B. Its precepts give life and liberty (45)

III. **IT IS A HELP IN TIME OF TROUBLE**
   A. It helps in time of despond (25)
   B. It aids when tempted with unrighteousness

IV. **ITS SAVING MESSAGE**
   A. Its expression (41)
   B. Its New Testament confirmation
      1. "Faith cometh by hearing. . ." (Rom. 10:17)
      2. "Search the Scriptures. . ." (John 5:39)

CONCLUSION:
The Word is a wonder.
The real wonder, however, is that we don't make more use of it.

CLEANSING A YOUNG MAN'S WAY

PSALM 119:9-11

INTRODUCTION:
The Bible is a most practical book. It speaks to the issues that touch on life. It shows how to deal with the problem of sin.

I.   **A PERTINENT PROBLEM (9a)**
    A. What is says
        1. "Wherewithall" — by what means
        2. "A young man" — one who is younger
        3. "Cleanse his way" — make it pure and upright
    B. What it means
        1. "How in the world can I keep my life what it ought to be?"
        2. Every young person needs to say that today (and all older people as well)

II. **A PERFECT PROVISION (9b)**
    A. The answer lies in the Word of God
        1. There are principles for every need
        2. Life must be patterned after Word
    B. This is a valid answer
        1. Any true morality in society based on the Word
        2. Those who deny Word want its precepts

III. **A PROBING PETITION (10)**
    A. "With my whole heart have I sought Thee"
    B. "Let me not wander from Thy commandments"

IV. **A PRACTICAL PRESENTATION (11)**
    A. The meaning of "hid" — to store up or to treasure
        1. Touches on value we put on Word
        2. Not enough just to memorize it
    B. A pallative for sin
        1. The Word and sin are the keys

2. Proper valuation of the Word will be decisive in the battle with sin
3. "The Word will keep you from sin, sin will keep you from the Word"

CONCLUSION:

Is it possible to live a clean and decent life in this evil world? The Word gives the perfect answer. The big question is — do you really want to?

WHAT TO DO
WHEN YOU ARE LIED ABOUT

PSALM 119:69

INTRODUCTION:
Salvation simplifies the inner life, but it can confuse the outer life. One of the upsetting things that hit us is the fact that we are sometimes lied about. Cheer up—it is nothing new—it happened in the Bible (David, Paul, early Christians, etc.) What should we do when it happens?

I. **BE SURE IT IS NOT TRUE**
   A. We are often blind to our own problems
   B. We do not like to admit the truth about ourselves
   C. If it is true, we need to correct the problem

II. **BE SURE YOU ARE NOT LYING ABOUT SOMEONE ELSE**
   A. Sow/Reap principle comes in at this point
   B. Does not make their lying right

III. **CONSIDER THE SOURCE**
   A. Some people just do not know any better
   B. Some people are clearly marked as liars and have no influence at all
   C. Some people are not worth fighting

IV. **IF YOU KNOW THE SOURCE, GO AND CONFRONT**
   A. It is always biblical to face issues with people
   B. Try to find out *why* as well as *what*
   C. Go in spirit of meekness—consider your own faults

V. **IF SOURCE AND EXTENT UNKNOWN, DO NOT ANSWER**
   A. Reason—if you do not answer everything, they will think part is true
   B. You give people satisfaction when you fight back

VI. IF SOURCE IS UNKNOWN, TRY TO IGNORE IT
A. Do not let it eat up your life
B. It is possible to ignore it

VII. TURN THE MATTER OVER TO GOD
A. Be sure you are doing right
B. Make it a matter of prayer
C. Give your reputation to God: let the attacks be against Him

VIII. LIVE ABOVE THE LIES
A. Maintain a right relationship with God
B. Do what is right regardless
C. Live in such a way as to make a lie show for what it is

IX. DO NOT EVER RESPOND IN KIND
A. We are actors, not reactors
B. Response in kind gives credence to charges and compounds problems

X. KEEP YOUR EYES ON CHRIST
A. He endured it
B. He went through it properly
C. He endured the contradiction of sinners as our example

CONCLUSION:
It is never pleasant to be lied about. It brings out the worst in us — defensiveness. Actually it is a real opportunity for spiritual growth.

THE GOD WHO IS THERE

PSALM 139:1-12

INTRODUCTION:
No one knows everything about anything or even anything about everything. The smartest of men still have mysteries with which to grapple. No one can be more than one place at a time. These limitations, however, do not apply to God. He is omniscient and omnipresent.

I. **DEFINITION**
    A. Omniscient: the capacity of knowing everything
    B. Omnipresent: the capacity of being everywhere at once
    C. Their relationship
       1. These two concepts are almost ways of expressing same thing—God knows everything because He is everywhere
       2. The two are hard to separate; the Psalmist runs them together

II. **DECLARATION (1-6)**
    A. Personalized "God knows me" (1)
    B. Particularized (2-5)
       1. He knows my sitting down and my rising up
       2. He knows my thoughts
       3. He surrounds my path and my "pad"
       4. He is familiar with all my habits, quirks, etc.
       5. He knows every word I use
       6. He is around me on every side
    C. Positionalized (6)
       1. The distance between the Lord and us is established by His closeness to us.
       2. Because You are far above me You are everywhere by me.

III. **DEMONSTRATION—TURNS TO OMNIPRESENCE (7-12)**
    A. Expression (7)

B. Extension: explores possibilities (8-10)
C. Expression: goes one step further (11, 12)

CONCLUSION (APPLICATIONS):
1. You should come to know the God who knows you
2. God's omniscience should caution us
3. God's omniscience should comfort us: He is the "God who is there!"

COMPREHENSIVE KNOWLEDGE

PSALM 139:1-6

INTRODUCTION:
We sometimes wonder if God knows what is going on. Things seem dark and hopeless; we would be reassured just to feel that He knows. Someone glibly says, "God knows all about it," but does He really? This passage has the answer.

I.   **THE THEME (1)**
   A.   The omniscience of God: "God knows all that has happened, all that is happening, and all that will happen as well as all that ever could"
   B.   The source of omniscience
      1.   The searching of God
      2.   Note words used to describe His searching: Know, understandeth, compasseth, acquainted, knowest

II.   **THE DEVELOPMENT (2-4)**
   A.   Extends to all the course of life (2a, 3a)
      1.   Relaxation activities
      2.   At home or away
      3.   "Thou art acquainted with all my ways" (3b)
   B.   Extends to the thought life (2b)
      1.   Everything that transpires in the mind
      2.   Thoughts are separated from motives
      3.   No geographical limitations
   C.   Extends to the area of speech (4)
      1.   Includes everything that is ever spoken
      2.   Forms the basis for His judgment

III.   **THE MEANING (5)**
   A.   The caution — "Thou hast beset me behind and before" (5a)
   B.   The guidance — "Thou hast laid Thine hand upon me" (5b)

IV. **THE REACTION (6)**
    A. Worship (6a)
        1. His knowledge is wonderful
        2. This provides us with an example
    B. Humility (6b)
        1. Recognition of God's superiority
        2. This is a healthy condition for us

CONCLUSION:
God knows all there is to know about us. This knowledge should make us watch
    Our steps
    Our thoughts
    Our words
It should also make us worship in a humble spirit.

THE PRESENCE OF GOD

PSALM 139:7-12

INTRODUCTION:
God is not located according to geography. He is everywhere. The theological term for this is "omnipresence." It has a lot of practical meaning and teaches us great truths.

I. **GOD'S OMNIPRESENCE PURSUES THE GUILTY IN HIS FLIGHT (7, 8)**
   A. Explanation
      1. The idea of flight: "go", "flee"
      2. The extent of flight: anywhere
      3. The failure of flight
   B. Illustration — Jonah
   C. Application
      1. God deals with flight
      2. Attempted flight is futile
      3. We can't escape God's presence

II. **GOD'S OMNIPRESENCE PROTECTS THE PERSECUTED ONE (9, 10)**
   A. Explanation — these verses are speaking of persecution
      1. "If I am driven to obscure places by persecution or troubles..."
      2. Helpful assurance
   B. Illustration — David himself (Ps. 3)
   C. Application
      1. There will be persecution
      2. There is power in persecution
      3. The presence of God is stronger

III. **GOD'S OMNIPRESENCE ASSURES US WHEN CRUSHED BY TROUBLE (11, 12)**
   A. Explanation: this deals with darkness, trials and troubles
   B. Illustrated — Elisha's servant in 2 Kings 6:13-17
   C. Applied

     1.   These are universal problems
     2.   God is always there

CONCLUSION:
The omnipresence of God means that He is everywhere:
You cannot flee with a guilty conscience
You cannot be chased out of His love by persecutors
You are loved and watched when depressed and crushed
   by problems
If you are running from God, it is entirely pointless to do so.

THANKS FOR THE MEMORIES

PSALM 145:7

I. **PRAYERS THAT HAVE BEEN HEARD (1)**
    "When" thou prayest, not "if"

II. **PETITIONS THAT HAVE BEEN HANDLED (2)**
    He handles so many requests

III. **PAINS THAT HAVE BEEN HEALED (3-5)**
    A. Salvation
    B. "We write our blessings in the sand and our burdens in marble."

IV. **PANICS THAT HAVE BEEN HELPED (6, 7)**
    1 Peter 5:10

V. **PATHS THAT HAVE BEEN HALLOWED (8, 9)**
    "Steps of a good man...." (Ps. 37:23)

VI. **PRACTICES THAT HAVE BEEN HONORED (10-18)**
    A. God's works praise Him (10)
    B. Take the cup of salvation and call on the name of the Lord. (11)
    C. Pay your vows to the Lord (14-18)
    D. Offer to God the sacrifice of thanksgiving (17)